Starting Your Own Sandwich Shop

by

Greg Jackson Rowe

"Starting Your Own Sandwich Shop" – Copyright © Greg Jackson Rowe 2012

Greg Jackson Rowe has asserted his right to be identified as the author of this work.

Appendices in this book written and researched by Max B. Powell. Copyright © Max B. Powell 2012

No part of this publication may be reproduced, stored in a retrieval system, or transmitted in any forms or by any means, electronic, mechanical, photocopying, recording or otherwise, without the prior permission of the copyright owner.

Disclaimer

The material in this book is for informational purposes only. Discretion should be used in all circumstances before undertaking any of the actions in this book. The author and publisher expressly disclaim any responsibility for any adverse effects from the use or application of any information contained within this book.

Contents

Introduction

Chapter 1 - Business Operations and Starting up	3
Chapter 2 - Commercial Premises and Hardware	9
Chapter 3 - Stock and Supplies	13
Chapter 4 - Taking Orders	15
Chapter 5 - Legal Requirements	17
Chapter 6 - Marketing and Promotion	20
Chapter 7 - Insurance	24
Chapter 8 - Customer Service	29
Appendix A - Trade Association/Trade News	31
Appendix B - Training	33
Appendix C - Health and Safety	36
Appendix D - Raising Finance	39
Appendix E - Managing your Money	42
Appendix F - Commercial Premises	45
Appendix G - Security	51
Appendix H - Marketing Tools	54

Starting your own sandwich shop

Introduction

This guide is for anyone looking to set up a sandwich shop and will outline all the necessary areas that have to be considered. There is also further essential information covered in the appendices at the end of the book.

Sandwich shops that are well located can make excellent revenue, and research shows that even with the recent economic downturn, sandwich shops continue to make money.

Research also indicates that many customers prefer a fresh tasting sandwich made on the spot rather than a pre-packaged one. A particular area of growth has been the corporate hospitality market, as companies seek sandwich delivery services to provide for their buffet lunches rather than more expensive hot meals.

Entry to the Market

Business advisors often refer to "barriers to entry", which is another way of describing the obstacles you might face in setting up a business. Each market sector will have a unique set of obstacles specific to that business sector in addition to more general barriers.

For a sandwich shop, the barriers aren't too great, but you will require knowledge of customer service, general business management skills, and an understanding of health and safety issues. There are no mandatory qualifications for setting up a sandwich shop, however your local authority may have compulsory food preparation courses that you'll need to attend.

The following chapters will take you through start up, daily operations, legislation, marketing/promotion, insurance selection and the all important customer service skills. The appendices cover areas that are common in the food retail business such as information on trade associations, training opportunities, finding a premises and raising finance.

Chapter 1 - Business Operations and Starting up

What are you selling?

It seems obvious but selecting a menu should be done with some thought as to what customers 'traditionally' want, and what you're uniquely able to provide, in order to differentiate from any competitors that happen to be located nearby. Searching the web will give you plenty of recipe ideas for sandwiches that you can then develop into your own style.

Build your menu around the thought that competitors could spring up at any time, and so aim to have a unique selling point (USP) to attract and keep customers. It doesn't have to be revolutionary, anything from just a simple twist on the type of fillings you offer, to the portion sizes, and the type of bread you use, can make a refreshing difference to your customers.

Some of the following questions need to be considered before a final decision on your menu is made however.

- What can you prepare and sell at an affordable cost, and still make a profit?

- What can be prepared in a hurry, should you run out of it?

- What ingredients can be stored long term (such as canned tuna)?

- Are you going to be baking your own bread/rolls/baps?

- How much of your budget can you allocate to stocking extras such as soft drinks, confectionary and crisps?

- Can you provide hot drinks like tea and coffee during a lunchtime rush?

- Can you provide hot fillings for your sandwiches (such as bacon and eggs) for breakfast customers?

The above factors will affect your cost control, your productivity and your customer service. Your menu will have to accommodate these factors as well as trying to build in a USP.

Some people may not like or be able to consume 'traditional' fillings, so what options are there for people with special dietary requirements?

- Will you be listing low fat/low salt/healthy options?

- Will you be selling 'soup in a cup'?

- How about sandwich alternatives like stuffed pitas and paninis?

- Will you be selling salads?

- What types of spread will you be using on your bread (butter, margarine, soft cheese or other alternatives)?

- What type of condiments and sauces can you stock and how many can you prepare yourself (like home made salsa)?

- Will you have a separate preparation space for vegetarian items?

Little extras like these can make a big difference to regular customers, who'll keep coming back for that special mayonnaise or extra soft bap.

Productivity

A great part of customer service is how quickly someone is served, and for you the more customers you can serve during a given day, means more money coming in. How many of your fresh made sandwiches can be pre-packed on site in anticipation of a lunch time rush? Can you take telephone orders and do you have space to store them until they're collected during lunch hour or some other allocated collection time?

What does all the above give us then? We have budget limits, the need for variety, and customer service requirements that will all dictate the shape of the menu.

As for the menu itself, we have the following options and ideas to consider:

- Sandwiches/Rolls/Baps - Bought in or baked on site

- Fillings - Cold and Hot

- Paninis

- Pitas

- Wraps

- Salads

- Vegetarian and other special dietary options
- Low fat/low calorie options
- Soup
- Variety of Spreads, Condiments and Sauces

Extras and drinks

- Soft Drinks
- Cakes/Muffins/Cookies/Pastries
- Confectionary
- Bottled Water
- Hot drinks like tea and coffee

Research Exercise

Make several sample menus and calculate the cost of each item. This should give you a better idea on the most cost effective menu as well as one that fits your vision. You can fine tune it once you're up and running.

Pricing

Your prices need to cover all your costs (fixed and variable costs) and also include a markup beyond them in order to make a profit. You may need to experiment a bit with the prices in the early days, before you're fully satisfied with the results. Being clear on your costs and how much of an impact they have is essential. Some of your costs will account for the same percentage per item (the individual ingredients), while other costs will have a reduced impact if you sell more of each item (overhead costs).

Reviewing the basics - Costs

Direct/Variable Costs - These are the costs associated with the actual production of your items, such as the ingredients used. Generally, they'll account for the same percentage cost per item (unless you start getting volume discounts from your suppliers).

Fixed Costs - These are costs that are commonly referred to as overheads, things such as rent, business rates, utilities, your salary, and insurance.

Reviewing the basics - Pricing

Percentage Mark up - This is the common way of pricing a product, where you add a percentage on top of your production costs. The mark up is made up of what profit you want to earn *plus* the fixed costs that the business incurs.

Making a final decision

Do some research by looking at what other businesses provide, and what is within *your* capabilities to provide. What can you do better than them? What can you offer that they don't provide? What competitive advantages can you develop into your menu?

Try out the menu options and calculate how much it costs to make each item. This will let you forecast how much stock to purchase and set pricing at a profitable level. Remember to take into account how much your competitors are charging as well, and if you can compete on price, then do so.

Prices charged will vary according to location, for example if you're based in a small town, prices will be significantly lower than if you were based in a big city or at a travel hub such as a train station or airport. Prices will also differ between a high street sandwich shop and one based in a shopping centre.

The final decision on pricing will be dependent on your market research and how well you can control your costs.

Chapter 2 - Commercial Premises and Hardware

Once you've decided on what you're going to be selling, you'll need to select a suitable premises and install all the fixtures that will support the business. The internal layout is as important as the size and location of a space. You may be restricted in how much modification you can do internally (as building changes will be subject to planning permission), so finding a space that is a close approximation in the first instance is your best bet.

Premises

The ideal location is one which is close to your potential customers and is also easy for regular customers to reach. (You also don't want it to be too far from where you reside either, unless you're willing to relocate!).

Your ultimate selection should be based on several factors:

Physical Location

- Proximity to lunchtime customers

- Proximity to passing traffic (such as shoppers, commuters, students).

- Ease of access and parking

- Ability to receive stock from suppliers

Layout and Space

- Store room & cold storage area

- Eating-in area (not essential but can be a plus to lunchtime customers looking for a place to sit and eat).

- Adequate area for customers to queue.

Don't limit your analysis to the above points or feel bound to them (delete items as you wish), as it's going to be difficult to find the ideal location that satisfies every requirement, however a focus on being close to your customers should be paramount.

For more information on finding and selecting a premises see the Appendix on "Commercial Premises", later in this book.

Fixtures

Your menu selection will dictate some of the fixtures and fittings you choose, however make sure to allocate yourself some space for future acquisitions, as and when you decide to alter or expand your menu.

Use the following as a guide to furnish your shop:

- Service Counter

- Sinks - double sinks, separate hand basin.

- Grills and toasters.

- Bakery oven - If you decide on baking some of your own loaves and other baked goods such as pasties and pizza slices. Remember though, you're supposed to be setting up a sandwich shop, not a bakery...

- Kettle, coffee maker, Tea urn.

- Soup urn.

- Freezer - for storage (and another for ice creams/ice lollies if you decide to stock them).

- Display counters and cases - including refrigerated units, drinks display units and chilled display cases.

- General kitchen equipment and utensils for food preparation and cooking, such as colanders, knives, pots and pans.

- Service cutlery such as butter knives and spoons or scoops for apportioning sandwich fillings.

Some items can be leased while others will have to be purchased. Once again, your budget is likely to dictate which option you choose.

Further Resources:

Visit the website of the Catering Equipment Suppliers Association for details of suppliers: www.cesa.org.uk

See the Shop and Display Equipment Association website for potential suppliers: www.shopdisplay.org, there may be costs involved on getting access to the information on this website (namely subscription fees).

Search the trade press classifieds for reconditioned items and foreclosure items; you don't have to buy brand new all the time. Beware of items that have had prolonged usage, subsequent repair costs may prove your new found bargain is anything but!

Food preparation, storage, and packaging items

Don't forget the items you'll be using on a daily basis such as the following:

- Deli tubs

- Takeaway packaging

- Disposable cutlery

- Napkins

- Carrier bags

The above can be purchased from either the Cash and Carry or the discount stores.

Search on the web and speak to your local grocer's and convenience stores for details of Cash and Carry outlets.

Chapter 4 - Handling Payments

You can't run a business unless you're taking in money and there are multiple methods of receiving payment. You'll find most people use cash and for this you'll need to make sure you have adequate amounts of change in your till. As for cheques, it's very rare these days that somebody would go into a sandwich shop to pay by cheque and it's your prerogative whether you accept one. For debit/credit card payments you'll require a card processing machine as well as a merchant account facility (obtainable via your bank).

Payment Facilities

To take cash payments you're going to need a cash till which will handle basic calculations and generate receipts. High-end cash machines (often referred to as point-of-sale machines) also allow you to monitor your stock levels and provide immediate feedback on your revenue. The other advantage to using high-end point of sales machines is that they will also tell you when a particular stock item is running low, giving you a heads up on what products need to be restocked.

Taking payment by card means you'll need a chip and pin machine to process them with. You have the option of either purchasing the machines or renting them. Renting the equipment may involve transaction fees on top of the monthly rental.

Go to the following websites for further details on cash registers:

- www.cashregistergroup.com

- www.cashregistersonline.co.uk

- www.cashtillsdirect.co.uk

- www.acetills.co.uk

- www.buyatill.com

It's worth speaking to your bank about your requirements as you may be able to acquire the machines directly through them. You'll certainly need to arrange merchant account/payment processing facilities via your bank and this can take time (anything up to 3 months), so speak to them as early as possible.

Chapter 5 - Legal Requirements

All businesses have to satisfy the statutory requirements for their business sector and these regulations may have minor additions/variations depending on your locality. Speak to your local authority and any relevant regulatory bodies at the earliest moment, and get yourself familiar with the guidelines and any certification process, to make sure you can satisfy all the expected requirements.

Registering and Establishing your Business

You must register your business with the Environmental Health Dept of your local council. Your application form has to be submitted before you open for business (usually at least 28 days beforehand, but check to see if there are any extra requirements for your local authority).

Website for information:

www.food.gov.uk/enforcement/enforceessential/startingup

Once you've registered, an inspection will be carried out by the environmental health officer. To ensure you pass satisfactorily, visit the Food Standards Agency website for information on food hygiene standards, where you should be able to find documentation covering businesses that sell food. Remember, regular visits will be conducted by the environmental health officer to ensure that you maintain standards and don't endanger any of your customers.

Legislation

Retail outlets selling food must adhere to the relevant legislation covering hygiene and safety.

The most relevant Acts are:

General Food Regulations Act 2004

Food Hygiene Regulations Act 2006

Food Labeling Regulations Act 1996

These acts cover everything from hygiene to food presentation. The Food Hygiene Regulation Act 2006 introduced the requirement for your shop to have in place a *"Food Safety Plan"* to aid in tracing the origin of any food contamination. Speak to Business Link, who'll be able to advise you of any further relevant regulations that could affect you.

Labelling regulations are covered by Food Labelling Regulations 1996. Pre-packaged food has to be labelled with the following information:

- Name of item

- Ingredients

- Best before dates

- Storage instructions

- Allergy information

- Details of the manufacturer/packer

These regulations are in place to prevent mishaps as well as to prevent the spread of any food poisoning incidents. Visit the Food Standards Agency website, www.food.gov.uk for further information on this legislation, and guidance on adhering to their requirements. Understanding the legislation will assist you in passing any inspections as well as ensuring training and operating standards are of a sufficient standard.

Chapter 6 - Marketing and Promotion

You've set up your shop and now you need to *actively* draw customers to you, as waiting for them to simply turn up won't create the results you're after. Even the most well known brand names will go on a marketing offensive when opening a new store or branch, and you should do the same. While you won't have the millions that they have available for marketing, there are plenty of tools you can utilise on even a small budget.

Marketing Tools

Signage

You can use A-boards to advertise outside your sandwich shop, however you may require permission before you put anything up. Check with your local authority to see what you need to obtain for putting up an A-board. If you have space out front which is part of your property, you may or may not need permission, but it's best to check with your local authority just in case.

Website

Your website could be used for advertising your shop and should include your menu, prices and location (plus directions) including the nearest place to park.

If you're feeling adventurous, you could also use it to take orders. The orders could either be collected in store or you could arrange for them to be delivered to your customer. Consider joining network websites like www.just-eat.co.uk as well, to further expand your web presence.

Just remember, there is legislation covering online food sales, for further information go to the Food Standards Agency website for information on Distance Selling Regulations.

Lunchtime Specials

Restaurants often use lunch time specials and lunchtime only menus to attract customers and there is no reason why you as a sandwich shop can't do the same. You can use a special 'lunchtime salad bar/buffet' or 'sandwich of the day' to attract new customers and to keep your regulars coming in more often. An advantage you hold over restaurants is that you'll be open for breakfast as well, and therefore can offer breakfast sandwiches, breakfast croissants, and deals on the morning coffee.

Meal Deals

Meal deals are used by many sandwich shops to up sell other products such as soft drinks and confectionary. A customer buying a sandwich is offered a discount for buying a combination of items, referred to as a meal deal (the customers save money buying the items together rather than individually). While you may be making a reduced margin on the items sold, what the customers have done for you though, is spend more money at your shop.

Ads in directories

Don't forget to have your shop listed in the Yellow Pages and other telephone directories, in both the online and off-line versions.

Special deals for students

Attract students looking for a bargain by offering discounts at your shop. This is where having a good location really helps, as being near to a school, college or university will pay dividends.

Loyalty scheme

You can set up a loyalty scheme for your regular customers. How you reward your regular customers is your choice, common examples are a free sandwich or a discount on a sandwich/meal deal after having purchased a set number of meals or items. Setting up a loyalty scheme also has the added bonus of encouraging more occasional customers to become regular customers. You could also offer informal discounts to regulars you recognise at your discretion.

Flyers

Flyers inserted into the local newspaper or handed out on the nearest corner or even outside your shop are common methods used by sandwich shops and takeaways to advertise their trade.

Samples

Offer customers the opportunity to sample your sandwiches, by giving passing shoppers and commuters the chance to try a selection from a sandwich platter. You may need to get permission from your local authority before you go out on to the streets to do the same thing.

Press Release

Send a press release to all your local papers and TV news channels. Hold an opening day with discounts for your sandwiches, making sure to have a 'Chef's Special'. Make sure you send out flyers advertising this to your local community as well. The local media are always looking for stories and your shop opening may be able to fill some space for them, which means free publicity for you. There's no harm in sending them a sample platter either!

Make it happen

Waiting passively for customers is not a strategy. While you'll still get customers coming in, you will attract far more by getting out there and making them aware of your shop and what it has to offer. Get into the habit of asking your customers how they heard about you. That way you'll be able to focus your efforts on the methods that work best for your shop.

Chapter 7 - Insurance

What if the worst happens? What if something catastrophic occurs that interrupts your business? How do you plan for it and more importantly what do you plan for, without becoming a nervous wreck over the slightest hiccup?

The good news is that such events are very rare and concerns about them shouldn't prevent you from starting a business of your own. Insurance cover has evolved to provide protection against most of the hiccups that might occur.

What to cover

Most businesses will take out a variety of different types of insurance cover to protect themselves against as many eventualities as possible. Injury, disease, death, damage to stock, damage to premises and vehicles, disruption to your business, and cover for theft are amongst the things you'll need to consider. Some types of cover are mandatory (such as Employer's Liability Insurance), while others such as life insurance, are not mandatory but are good to have if you can stretch your budget. Assessing your risks on a regular basis, ideally once per quarter, to ensure you're not exposed is good practise.

Consider the following areas where mishaps could occur:

Individuals

- Your customers and the general public: accidental injury related to your business.

- Yourself: illness and injury preventing you from working.

- Employees: accidental injury or death related to your business.

Business Operations

- General incidents on your commercial premises such as fire, theft, and accidental damage

- Incidents involving any commercial vehicles you own and use.

- Mishaps during deliveries; (should you be running a delivery service for your products as well).

The following is a list of the types of cover that you could take out against these eventualities:

- Liability Insurance (Public Liability, Product Liability, Professional Indemnity, Personal Liability)

- Employers Liability Insurance. (Compulsory)

- General Commercial Insurance

- Vehicle Insurance (Compulsory; you should consider commercial vehicle insurance, as standard vehicle insurance may not cover all possibilities).

- Buildings and Content Insurance

- Goods in transit Cover (for deliveries)

- Life Insurance/Income Protection/Critical Illness (for you).

- Business Equipment Cover.

- Business Interruption Cover.

- Legal Expenses Insurance.

- Key Man Insurance (usually only used in large corporations)

- Credit Insurance (protect against debtors failing to pay you).

The decision on what to cover and to what extent is largely up to the individual business. Apart from the mandatory cover that you'd need, the rest will depend upon your budget and to what extent you feel you can absorb the costs of any accidents should you decide not to select cover for a particular eventuality.

Selecting what range of insurance to purchase should be relatively easy, but it's worth speaking to a professional, such as an Insurance Broker who can provide advice on the type of cover you'd need.

Finding a Broker

Brokers in any trade are the middle men (and women) who act as a point of contact between service suppliers and service consumers. They use their knowledge to provide you with a suitable product, reducing your need to run around looking for the right deal.

An independent broker can give you unbiased advice on a range of options and guide you on what is suitable to your business. They should be able to advise you on the limitations of a particular policy, assist you in making a claim, and point out methods you can implement to help bring down the premium you pay.

Speak to a broker who specialises in commercial insurance, that way you'll receive information which is tailored to your business. You can find a broker using the resource list below as a starting point.

Resource List

The organisations below will have valuable information and lists of members which you can view.

- The British Insurance Brokers Association (BIBA) - www.biba.org.uk, is one place where you can find a broker. Search for commercial insurance and possibly look for specialist cover in your particular trade.

- The Association of British Insurers - www.abi.org.uk, is a trade association for insurance companies in the UK.

- There is also a professional organisation for insurance brokers called The Institute of Insurance Brokers - www.iib-uk.com.

When choosing a broker, consider if they specialise in your area of business, what size businesses they are used to dealing with, and whether its cost effective to use one. You may find that you can effectively purchase the cover directly from an insurer without the need for a broker. Many larger insurers are easy to deal with, thus dispensing the need to use a broker at all. Either way, visit several brokers and get quotes from them before making a final decision.

Selecting a Policy

Whether you select from a range of different types of cover or a specialist package, you'll need to do some background work before making a final decision. Verify any insurance company you select by checking their details with the Financial Services Authority (website - www.fsa.gov.uk).

You could also obtain specialist insurance cover for your business via your market sector's trade association, however this may only be available to members of the association, (in which case you'll have to join and pay their subscription fees first). Alternatively, being a member of an association could entitle you to discounts with some firms.

Ask others for recommendations on brokers and insurance companies as well, speak to local business owners, and friends and family who may own businesses. While price is a factor when selecting cover, you should also consider how easy it is to get in touch with the insurer and what their claims process is like. The last thing you want is to be stuck on the phone while trying to resuscitate your business after a major event!

Chapter 8 - Customer Service

You're nothing without your customers, keep that in mind at all times. I'm sure we can all recall instances of poor customer service, where we've been left with a feeling that a particular business saw us as nothing more than a nuisance that needs to be tolerated. Chances are you didn't deal with them any further after that experience.

Just as likely, we can all recall instances of great customer service, where an employee has gone out of their way to help us, way beyond their job description, just to make sure we got what we were after. Their efforts persuaded you to use their services again after that.

Which of the above scenarios will get more regular customers? Which of the above will have a more pleasant working environment? After all if you don't like your workplace, this gets reflected in your attitude towards your customers.

Building a customer base of regulars is absolutely essential if you intend to be in business for a long time. While it's always important to bring in new sales, your focus should be geared to making as many regular customers out of these new sales.

Give customers what they want

The data you gain from market research and your own sales data will build a picture of what your customers like and what will then bring in more customers. Monitoring what is selling well and contrasting this with background information, such as the time of sale and the type of customer (office worker at lunch, shopper passing by, student, tourist etc) will help you define a strategy to attract regular customers. This feedback from your sales is absolutely essential to developing and fine tuning your strategy, and it will also help make sure you stock the right products, rather than waste money on a wide range of goods which may not sell.

Building Loyalty

Be easy to deal with. If a customer is unhappy, give them a refund or replacement without them having to jump through hoops. News of your good nature and friendly service will soon spread to others. A social connection goes a long way in turning an occasional customer into a regular customer and becoming a focal point during their day guarantees regular visits. Building your customer base in this way helps protect you against any new competitors that might pop up. To displace you they'll need to do more than what you are already doing.

You may have heard the phrase, "sell the sizzle, not the sausage", and it refers to the method of attracting customers via an emotional connection rather than a logical buying decision. How a person feels when making a purchase and how they feel after having made a purchase is important in building loyalty. They will seek to repeat the positive experience on more occasions and this means more business for you.

Consider the businesses you purchase from repeatedly, why do you use them and how could you mirror their methods in your own business?

Appendix A - Trade Association/Trade News

There are trade specific sources of information which can help to keep you abreast of the latest trends and events happening in your market sector. Trade associations if available, also provide other benefits to their members, ranging from access to cheaper insurance to legal advice. Membership costs can also vary to suit every type of budget.

Trade Associations:

British Sandwich Association. Website: www.sandwich.org.uk

National Catering Association. Website: www.ncass.org.uk

Despite the name, the NCASS is open to membership from sandwich shops.

Publications:

International Sandwich & Snack News is the magazine of the British Sandwich Association. Go to the website: www.sandwich.org.uk for more details.

Websites:

www.sandwichnews.com

www.just-food.com

BSA Code of Practise:

The British Sandwich Association has a code of practice for members selling sandwiches made on site. Visit their website for details of their latest best practice guidelines.

Appendix B - Training

While training is not mandatory, there are organisations from whom you may obtain relevant training for you and your staff should you wish to do so.

General Training

- Chartered Institute of Health - website: www.cieh.org

    The CIEH offer food safety courses for both the retail and catering sector, covering topics on avoiding food contamination and supervisory skills.

- Nationwide Caterers Association - website: www.ncass.org.uk

    The NCASS provide online training courses for food safety skills

Catering Management Courses

For courses on catering management approach your nearest further education college or go to the City & Guilds website: www.cityandguilds.com for information.

Online Self study courses

Low cost online self study courses are also available from a variety of sources. Learn Direct may have some courses of interest to you.

Learn Direct website: www.learndirect.co.uk

The site offers courses covering such topics as retail, sales, customer service and marketing.

Your local library may also have access to online learning resources and they're likely to be free.

General Business skills courses

The Institute of Leadership and Management (ILM) and the Chartered Management Institute (CMI) both offer management courses that are recognised for their standards. The courses are pricier than the online courses available elsewhere, but for those of you with no management/supervisory experience and who feel you need some training, it's a good place to start. They can't replicate real experience in the catering trade however, and the cost of the courses may be a deciding factor.

The Institute of Leadership and Management Website: www.i-l-m.com

Chartered Management Institute Website: www.managers.org.uk

Further information:

The Food Standards Agency also provides guidance on food hygiene via their website.

See www.food.gov.uk for guides on regulations and advice.

Appendix C - Health and Safety

Health and safety is an essential item for a food retailer. Working in close cooperation with your local environmental heath team will ensure you manage your business without any problems. A health and safety assessment will be a statutory requirement for your business. Visit the website of the Health and Safety Executive (HSE) for more information about fulfilling your obligations.

Hygiene

After a long day of service, you'll need to clean your shop thoroughly, which means purchasing cleaning equipment and cleaning products. Check with the Food Safety Agency for any products to avoid and which ones are deemed essential. Make sure you gain a clear understanding of the level of cleanliness expected so you can budget for cleaning products. For example, you shouldn't use the same mop for both your bathroom/w.c. and your shop front/dining area (which means purchasing two sets of mops and buckets).

The decision on where you source your supplies will also be dictated by your budget and available storage space. Therefore, get familiar with the different potential suppliers to keep abreast of the latest prices and offers.

Safety at work

Any businesses using cleaning materials and sharp tools have to provide staff with the appropriate clothing and equipment, to reduce and prevent the possibility of serious injury. Staff have to be trained adequately in the use of any potentially dangerous equipment. Make yourself aware of your legal obligations to any employees you have.

Waste Disposal and Removal

Relevant Legislation - Environmental Protection Act 1990

Food preparation will generate a large amount of waste, and this is the type of waste that if improperly disposed of, will quickly deteriorate and cause all types of problems for yourself and your neighbours.

Some catering waste will require disposal by an authorised waste disposal company, who will remove any waste and dispose of it at an approved location. Check with your local authority's environmental health department on what the requirements are for your location and type of business. Visit the following 2 websites for further information:

The Environment Agency; www.environment-agency.gov.uk/netregs

Department for Environment, Food and Rural Affairs (DEFRA) - www.defra.gov.uk

Fire Safety

Fire is a genuine hazard for a food retailer, and adequate measure need to be taken to keep you, your staff and your customers safe. Fire blankets and fire extinguishers have to be in positions of easy access, fire escapes have be clearly identifiable and usable at all times. Check the HSE (Health and Safety Executive) website for a full set of recommendations and statutory requirements.

PAT Testing

PAT testing is done on portable electrical items that are plugged into the mains and the test is designed to ensure they are safe to use. As the business owner, it's your duty to have all appliances tested. Visit www.pat-testing.info for further information. (PAT stands for Portable Appliance Testing).

Appendix D - Raising Finance

Finance (or the lack of) and perceived budget size seem to be the most common reasons for NOT starting a business. It needn't be that way as there are plenty of options available which can assist you in boosting your budget.

While *there is no guarantee* that you'll be able to get any *formal* help from anyone at the very start, it's worth doing some research into finding out what's possible *informally*, and what may become also available once your business is up and running. When it comes to raising funds, a well researched business plan and a great imagination make the perfect combination to solve the problem.

Below is a list of possibilities:

- Personal Savings

- Informal Loans from friends and family

- Banks - Overdrafts, loans, Credit cards

- Private equity - Venture capital (investment in exchange for equity in your company), Business Angels (private investors looking to invest in other businesses)

- Government Funding- Early Growth Fund, Grants, local authority development funding (details vary, speak to your local authority).

- Business support organisations - Enterprise agencies, The Princes Trust, Charitable Organisations.

- Commercial Services - Asset Financing (a loan secured on an asset you require for business), Factoring and Invoice discounting (payments made to you by your bank in advance of receiving payments on invoices you've issued, details will vary, your business may need to be of a certain size and corporate structure to qualify).

To obtain financing of any kind you'll need a thoroughly researched business plan. It has to be convincing enough to any potential finance providers to justify their input.

Summary

It's easy to *think* yourself out of a business opportunity due to a perceived lack of funds. Your business plan will pinpoint the level of startup capital required, and the guidance above should give plenty of ideas in how to raise these funds.

Have a search on the following websites for further information.

Web resources - this is just a sampling of what is available out there:

UK Angel Investors - www.angelinvestorsnetwork.co.uk

British Business Angels - www.bbaa.org.uk

Enterprise Agencies - www.nationalenterprisenetwork.org

The Prince's Trust - www.princes-trust.org.uk

British Venture Capital Association - www.bvca.co.uk

Government Funding - visit the business link website - www.businesslink.gov.uk

Appendix E - Managing your money

Money management can appear daunting at first and so can the rest of your accounting needs. It needn't be that way and while a single chapter can't possibly cover everything, we can go over the basics to give you a better idea of what's expected of you.

Business Bank Account

You'll need a business bank account to process your revenue and keep it separate from your personal finances and expenditure. Most banks will give new accounts free banking facilities for the first 12-18months as well.

It's preferable to go in with a business plan when you see them, and there will be some due diligence procedures for the bank to carry out before they open an account for you, (getting an understanding of how you'll be making money, visiting your premises, and speaking to you about your sales expectations). It will probably be easier to open an account with a bank that you already hold a personal account with.

It's rare for a bank to provide credit facilities (credit card or overdraft) to a new business account, although you should receive your account debit card within a week and a cheque book/paying in book soon after that. If you are expecting to receive foreign currency, make sure your account can accept this and also confirm electronic transfers and direct debit payments facilities are available.

Should you be processing credit/debit card payments, you'll need merchant account facilities through your bank, as well as a card processing machine if you're physically authorising them (and not just processing via an ecommerce website). Your bank will be able to discuss security procedures with you in regards to card payments and online banking.

Accounting Software and Accountants

Keeping track of you expenditure and revenue is easier when using account software. Expect to pay £99 and upwards, unless you decide to use spreadsheet software such as excel, which you may already have on your computer. Sample spreadsheet templates can be obtained free online. You may need to print invoices and receipts via your software, so check what options the accounting software has and if you can customise the templates to suit your business.

Another option is to hire a bookkeeper to manage your books for you. They don't have to be on staff with you, as there are plenty of people who freelance in this field. If you have a Limited Company, you'll need to submit accounts on a regular basis via a Chartered Accountant.

When choosing an accountant it's best to go with a recommendation from someone you trust such as a friend, business owner or bank contact.

Taxes

Get in touch with the Inland Revenue (now known as the HMRC, www.hmrc.gov.uk) about getting registered for tax and what your liabilities are. Speak to Business Link for advice on your particular business structure, and consult with an accountant if you can.

Make sure you understand when your tax year starts and finishes, and when your tax return is due. There are significant differences between a Limited Company and being a Sole Trader/Self Employed.

National Insurance is also payable, (there are different levels if you're self employed), and depending on your business structure/market sector and expected revenue levels, you may also need to register for VAT.

While there are plenty of books on this subject, changes happen frequently so it's best to get advice directly from the experts.

Summary

Get advice from business owners you may know, from Business Link (www.businesslink.gov.uk), your bank, and from the HMRC. Keep meticulous records of your finances and keep all your receipts, making sure you have backup copies.

Speak to an accountant if you are having difficulties with your financial calculations, (make sure they're experienced in your trade). Speak to your bank about what support they can provide and any recommendations on finding an accountant, after all it's in their interest that you succeed.

Appendix F - Commercial Premises

Finding the right location initially seems straightforward and then quickly starts to look complicated once you see all the options that are available, from the type of building to the method of occupancy. The other daunting factor can be all the different costs involved in acquiring, moving into and maintaining your property.

Hopefully after reviewing this chapter you'll be better aware of the options available to you and what is most suited to your budget and type of business.

Budget

Your budget needs to be able to cover the initial costs of acquiring a place as well as ongoing costs. The building is likely to need modification to make it suitable for its intended purpose, so you'll need to factor in costs for repair and refurbishment, plus equipment costs.

On top of this, there will be stamp duty and professional/legal fees to pay. You may need to use a property surveyor to advise you on your plans for refurbishment and a law firm to deal with your contracts, (legal advice is essential before signing anything).

Then there are the ongoing costs such as rent/mortgage, business rates, service charges and the cost of maintenance. Will your business bring in enough revenue to cover these costs?

Finding the right location

Finding the right location is not that difficult, no matter what people may tell you. You will need to put in the time and effort to find a place however, and you can expect to make plenty of phone calls during your search.

Places to begin your search are:

- Commercial Property Agents. Register with several commercial property agents to maximize your chances of finding the right place. Visit your local real estate agents as they often have commercial departments as well.

- Web search: There are now a variety of property websites offering commercial properties of all types. Some specialise in a particular field while others mix residential and commercial.

- Legwork: Visit areas where you are interested in setting up your business, to see if there are any properties for sale or let. This also gives you the opportunity to collect the contact details of property agents from their advertising boards.

- Speak to your friends, family and the owners of business whom your familiar with. They may know someone or may have seen an empty/disused property.

- The Business Centre Association, website - www.bca.uk.com, will have listings for managed and serviced office space and industrial units.

- The property section of your local newspaper.

Before you start your hunt, plan out what your business needs and how you'll physically arrange everything on your site. This will give you a better idea of the type of location that will fit your needs. Make sure you have accurate measurements of all the equipment and furnishings that you intend to install.

Making a decision

Once you've found several possible locations, you'll need a way to decide which one is most suitable. The criteria used is obviously going to be dependent on the type of business you intend to run, however the following are other common points to consider:

- Accessibility: Can your customers get in to your premises easily? Can you receive deliveries without disrupting you business or your neighbours?

- Proximity: How close to your customer base are you? Is it easy to travel to your location?

- Discoverability: Are you easily spotted from the street? Will passing traffic notice you and is there somewhere close by for them to stop?

- Competition: How many potential competitors are there close by? Is this a positive or a negative for you, (shoppers naturally congregate to a shopping mall or high street)? Can you use this existing target market to draw in new customers?

Research regarding the premises

Along with these factors are the legislative hurdles you'll need to negotiate. Your business may not be permissible within the area you've chosen or you could be subject to regulations that may hinder your business or prevent future expansion. There will also be health and safety concerns to consider, along with ensuring access for people with reduced mobility or physical disabilities. Check the details of these with your local authority and with the present owner/property agent of the building.

Hiring the services of a Chartered Surveyor will also ensure everything is right with the building and they'll also go over your plans with you.

For information on Chartered Surveyors, visit the website of The Royal Institute of Chartered Surveyors - www.rics.org

Buying or Leasing

Buying:

If you have the capital and are confident in your plans, you could buy your own property. Having your own property gives you more freedom than you would have, if you decided to rent or lease a property.

Leasing:

You can obtain a lease either directly from the freeholder's property agent or arrange to have a lease transferred to your name directly from the present leaseholder (an "assigned lease"). Make sure to read the small print on your lease, as to what changes you can make (if any) to the interior, what equipment you can install, what type of business you're allowed to operate, and any restrictions on opening hours. (Note: Leases can't be terminated in advance without setting the terms of any cancellation, *before signing your agreement*).

Licensed Occupancy:

If you're looking for a short term site and are happy with sharing facilities, a licensed occupancy could be for you. You're more likely to have this option when looking for an office rather than a retail outlet however.

Managed/Serviced Units:

These types of units have the advantage of being ideal for short term use, especially if you're unsure of how successful you may be and therefore don't want to be tied down to a commercial mortgage or lease. The owner of the property will have arranged connection for all essential services already, (utilities, security, telephone, internet access etc), giving you the chance to move in quite rapidly. There may also be shared facilities such as a cafeteria, reception desk and access to meeting rooms, giving you all the trappings of a larger organisation.

This type of property is rarely suitable for retail outlets and they are usually not located near a high street either. There are often limits on how long you may hire space in these units, so it's imperative to search for a long term solution while you get your business on its feet.

Some sites also operate as 'business incubators', providing networking opportunities and advice to new entrepreneurs. Speak to Business Link (www.businesslink.gov.uk) for further advice on finding the closest incubator site or try My Incubator (www.myincubator.co.uk) for more information on this service. The Business Centre Association, (www.bca.uk.com), will have listings for managed and serviced office space and industrial units.

Business Rates

Business rates are decided by your local authority and are payable to them. They are calculated on a mix of factors including things such as the size of the property, location and business use.

Under certain circumstances you may be liable for business rates even when working from home, however this depends on the type of business set up that you have, and the number of people working for you.

Service Charges

Service charges are payable to a property management company (if your located in a unit within a larger building and it's serviced in any way). The fees are used for the upkeep of common areas such as the car park, elevators, stairwells and general cleanliness etc.

Summary

The final choice you make will be limited by what is available and what you can afford. Aim for a site within easy reach of your customer base, ideally with plenty of 'passerby' traffic, who may come in on an impulse (if it's a retail outlet) or one with close access to transport hubs and parking, if it's an office based organisation.

Appendix G - Security and Data Protection

After all the hard work you put into setting up your business, it's a good idea to seek some form of protection for it, and depending on the type of business you run some of the following methods may also be a legal requirement.

Data Protection

If you store information on your customers for any length of time, you may need to register with the Information Commissioners Office (website - www.ico.gov.uk). This registration has to be renewed annually and there is a small fee to pay. Visit their website to find out how to comply with the Data Protection Act.

Alarms

Alarms act as a deterrent as well as providing an alert when a break-in occurs. Get an alarm system which is monitored remotely to ensure a quick response.

CCTV

Cameras can act as a deterrent to potential criminals as well as assist in the investigation of any crimes. As you will be recording private individuals you will need comply with the CCTV Code of Practice as outlined by the Information Commissioners Office. (website - www.ico.gov.uk).

Safe

A safe is a requirement to hold cash (and other valuable items) until you can deposit it at the bank. You can obtain one from office supply stores and locksmiths.

Security Shutters

Security shutters aren't the most aesthetic of items but are seen as essential in some areas. Some are mechanical and need to be hand wound/shut while others are electrically controlled.

Door Supervision and Security Guards:

Security guards are usually used in larger retail stores while door supervisors are usually only present in nightclubs, bars and some pubs. Any security personnel will need to have had the appropriate training and hold the necessary licensing as well.

Make sure all security staff understand what your expectations of them are, and how you wish your patrons/customers to be treated. You can either hire staff from security firms or on a freelance basis.

Police Contact:

Speak to your local police service on advice specifically for your type of business, and how to contact them for non-emergencies.

Further Resources:

Visit the website of the British Security Industry Association to find suppliers of the above items, www.bsia.co.uk

Appendix H - Marketing Tools

What is your Marketing Strategy?

No matter the size of your business, a marketing strategy will focus your efforts along a well defined and clear path, leading to sustained profitability. The lack of a marketing strategy results in the spending of cash on efforts that may not bring any benefit to your business. A strategy will define the direction you should be taking with your marketing, and make efficient and effective use of your marketing budget.

Your goals are to penetrate a particular market, and promote your goods and services. To this end, measurable targets have to be set in order to gauge the effectiveness of your marketing plan. The results from this can then be used to modify your plan and to achieve the goals set by your strategy.

Developing your Marketing Plan

Your marketing plan takes your marketing objectives and combines them with the actions needed to complete them and sets out a prospective timeframe for these actions. Together, they create a roadmap of where you want to go, and how you're going to get there. The five steps to designing your plan are:

- Defining who is buying from you.

- Identifying what is your market niche.

- Developing your image.

- Selecting which marketing mediums to use.

- Getting the most from your marketing budget.

Who is buying from you?

Knowing who buys (or will be buying) your goods/services is the first step to designing your marketing plan. Without this knowledge you could find yourself trying to sell something for which there isn't a market, "Build it, and they will come" is not an effective strategy to start with!

Before you get to the meat and bones of your planning, you need to understand thoroughly why customers would buy from you and not someone else.

Questions to ask include:

- Is there a gap in the market that you can exploit?

- Are potential customers travelling far to other places and could you provide a service closer to home for them?

- Who is buying from your competitors?

- What is the social and economic background of these customers?

- How do you get customers to buy from you rather than your competitors?

A thorough review of these will take you to the next step in developing your plan.

What is your market niche?

Your market can be divided into smaller segments to make it easier to design a marketing plan, and also make the plan more accurate through better and relevant targeting, and thus more effective. You can divide your market from two perspectives; demographic perspective (who are you selling to) and product perspective (what is special about your products/services).

Demographic profiling is dividing your market by age, occupation, income level, and gender. For example: students, "blue collar" workers, "white collar" workers, and other professionals, who will all have distinct (though sometimes overlapping) cultural lifestyles and interests.

Within these groups, you can further sub-divide by lifestyle choices. This will be difficult to do for some businesses as gathering such data will not always be possible. Getting knowledge of how they make their purchasing decisions, whether they are financially independent, how they form opinions, and what emotions drive them, is only feasible for large businesses with schemes such as loyalty points cards (via data mining of information from purchasing habits), and who can also commission market research surveys.

The other approach to consider is from a product perspective. This is where you identify how your business fits into the market. Are the products and services you provide 'mainstream' or 'niche'? Are you specialising in a certain area of your market? For example, you could be aiming your products at one gender, age group, or your products themselves could be centred around a theme. Are you filling a gap in the market with your product?

Once you've identified the different niches in your market, you can create a plan to exploit this knowledge. Your next step is to project your presence into the market and for that you'll need a distinct and identifiable image.

Developing your image

A distinct image lets you stand out against a market where there may be many competitors or where your unique selling point is not immediately obvious to potential customers.

Your aim is to present your business as the answer to the customer's problem (whether that's "what to have for lunch" or "who to buy insurance from"), and explain how they will benefit more by using you, over any of your competitors.

Your image will attract your customers as well as give your marketing plan something to use as a 'centre of gravity' around which your promotional efforts can revolve. Protecting and polishing it as your business develops will further improve the results from these marketing efforts.

What marketing media to use?

The answer to this is 'as many as is possible'! Using as many different forms of media in a targeted manner, will ensure you reach all those valuable customers. However, your budget (and imagination) may limit the number of different forms you select. There is a list of possibilities at the end of this chapter.

While you want to reach as many people as possible, to be cost effective however, use the media that is most likely to be seen by your target customer. Remember, go to where your customers are, don't wait for them to come to you.

Marketing Budget

Your budget needs to compare the potential revenue possible, against the minimum cost of each marketing tool. This will give you an idea on how much you can spend on marketing and how cost effective each method is likely to be. If you see that the cost of a particular tool won't give you a positive return for the level of sales you're expecting, than it's probably best not to try it at that stage.

Adapting to changing circumstances

All plans need to change as the circumstances they were designed for continue to change. Don't slavishly follow a plan based on some perceived perfection, no matter how long you worked on it. If it's no longer relevant to the situation, it won't work anymore.

Fluctuations in your business require measured responses that are based on statistics. Monitoring and reviewing regularly, rather than at irregular intervals, will provide a wealth of reliable data, from which you can create a calculated plan of action.

Reviewing your plan on a monthly basis is a good idea, as well as planning actions for a variety of different possibilities. Based on the feedback received, you'll be in a good position to target your marketing plan towards your business objectives (as outlined in your marketing strategy).

Methods

How you promote your business is limited only by your imagination. There are options available for every budget,

Offline Methods

The traditional methods of advertising for business (such as window displays and signs, A-boards and banners) can be effective at getting passing trade through your door. To really make an impact, you'll need to go to where the customers are and where they're likely to search for a business such a yours. To make yourself standout from the rest of the crowd once you're there, you'll have generate a 'buzz' around your business. This requires you to do things your competitors aren't currently doing, and things that will also get people telling their friends about your business (in a good way!).

Online methods

While many people assume online advertising is more suited to non-localised businesses/ecommerce only businesses, the web can actually bring people to your business even if it's a locally focussed one, as more and more people are searching for what they're after via the web. Whether it's someone looking for a place to stay or eat, somewhere close by to get their hair done, get a gadget fixed, or just a place for the monthly staff night out, it's often the case that people will search on the internet first, (especially now in the age of smartphones, making search much more convenient). Having an online presence can help to draw those extra few customers to your business.

Below is a list of ideas that won't cost the earth to try out.

- Ads in print media
- Leaflets/Flyers
- Yellow Pages
- Posters
- Street Banners

- Promotional events (free samples/free membership)

- Special Offers and discounts such as Buy one, get one free (BOGOF)

- Loyalty Schemes

- Press releases

- Charity sponsorship

- Event Sponsorship

- Website

- Blogs and Articles

- PPC Ads

- Using social media (such as facebook and twitter)

The above list is only a starting point, use it to brainstorm more ideas that you can then build into a marketing plan.